Touring the

with the Fred Harvey Co. & the Santa Fe Railway

Paul and Kathleen Nickens

Schiffer Publishing Ltd

4880 Lower Valley Road Atglen, Pennsylvania 19310

Dedication

To our children, Lisa, Laura, and Gregory, who spent their childhoods traveling with us throughout the Southwest – heartfelt thanks to each of you for those precious memories.

Schiffer Books are available at special discounts for bulk purchases for sales promotions or premiums. Special editions, including personalized covers, corporate imprints, and excerpts can be created in large quantities for special needs. For more information contact the publisher:

Schiffer Publishing Ltd.
4880 Lower Valley Road
Atglen, PA 193106
Phone: (610) 593-1777
Fax: (610) 593-2002
E-mail: Info@schifferbooks.com

For the largest selection of fine reference books on this and related subjects, please visit our web site at **www.schifferbooks.com.** We are always looking for people to write books on new and related subjects. If you have an idea for a book please contact us at the above address.

This book may be purchased from the publisher. Include $5.00 for shipping. Please try your bookstore first. You may write for a free catalog.

In Europe, Schiffer books are distributed by:
Bushwood Books
6 Marksbury Ave.
Kew Gardens
Surrey TW9 4JF England
Phone: 44 (0) 20 8392-8585
Fax: 44 (0) 20 8392-9876
E-mail: info@bushwoodbooks.co.uk
Website: www.bushwoodbooks.co.uk
Free postage in the U.K., Europe; air mail at cost.

Contents

4

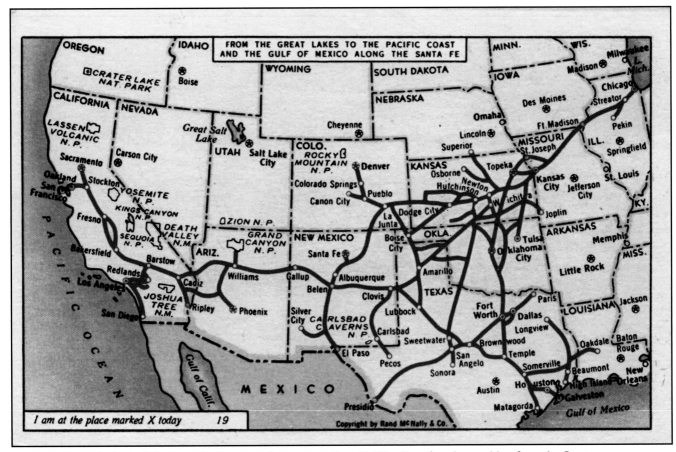

From the back: "The Santa Fe System embraces more than 13,100 miles of track stretching from the Great Lakes, west to the Pacific Coast, and South to the Gulf of Mexico and the Mexican border." Pre-1930; $6-8

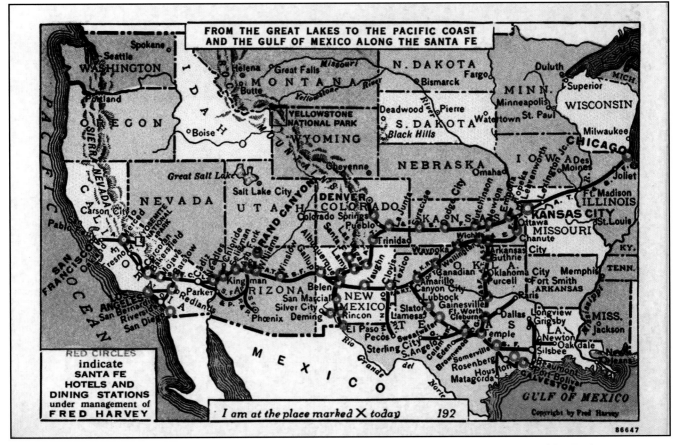

Map postcard indicating the locations of Santa Fe hotels and dining stations under management of the Fred Harvey Company along the Santa Fe Routes. Pre-1930, Fred Harvey No. 86647; $6-8

⊙ Introduction

A watershed episode in the growth of tourism in Arizona and New Mexico followed the coming of the Santa Fe Railway and restaurants run by the Fred Harvey Company. When completed in the mid-1880s, the Santa Fe mainline route extended from Chicago, Illinois, westward to Los Angeles, California. The Santa Fe line soon dominated transcontinental travel to the Southwest and helped to ignite the southern California population boom of the era.

The Santa Fe's line followed the Old Santa Fe Trail of historical fame across the plains of Kansas into southeastern Colorado. At the Colorado-New Mexico border, the route crossed the summit of Raton Pass, breaching the Rocky Mountain plateau, and passed through New Mexico and Arizona in an east-west transect. Exiting Arizona over the Colorado River at Needles, California, the course crossed the California desert, over Cajon Pass, and into the luxuriant San Gabriel Valley and Los Angeles basin.

Accompanying the rail route was the Fred Harvey Company. Led by the entrepreneurial spirit of Frederick Henry Harvey, who emigrated from London in 1850 at the age of 15, the Harvey Company formed a mutually beneficial partnership with the Santa Fe Railway beginning in the late 1870s, offering food and lodging along the route. By the early 1900s, the Harvey Company operated in dining cars on the track and in numerous eating houses and hotels at stops along the rail route.

To promote travel to the Southwest, the Santa Fe vigorously publicized the region's cultures, scenery, healthy climate, and real estate opportunities. As the Harvey Company expanded in the Southwest after 1900, it too advertised the natural and cultural qualities of the area. Working together to inspire the nation's traveling public, the Santa Fe Railway and Fred Harvey Company marketed the Southwest through advertisements placed in mass media, illustrated booklets, calendars, lithographs, playing cards, and postcards. They ran illustrated lectures, displays of Native American artifacts and architectural elements, craft demonstrations, dances, Indian sales rooms, side tours to Indian villages and natural wonders, and displays of paintings by noted western artists.

Postcards were particularly important as graphic representations of the Southwest experience and served as vehicles for sharing one's experience in this "Land of Enchantment." In addition to being inexpensive, postcards were easily collected and arranged into albums. Because of their popularity, the Fred Harvey Company produced a wide assortment of postcard images depicting cultural aspects of the region. Harvey postcards also highlighted the roles of the Santa Fe line and Harvey company, including the trains, hotels, eating houses, and other ventures.

A Note on Postcard History and Pricing

The use of postcards in the United States postal system goes back to the 1870s. For this study, postcards published between 1900 and 1950 are most important. Postcard history during this timeframe can be subdivided into five identifiable printing type eras:

Pre-1907, Undivided Back Era – 1901 to March 1, 1907
Pre-1915, Divided Back Era – 1907 to 1915
Pre-1930, White Border Era – 1915 to 1930
Pre-1945, Linen Card Era – 1930 to 1945
Pre-1960, Modern Photochrome Era – 1939 to 1960s
(Standard Size, 3½" x 5½")

Most of the postcards included in this volume were published under the Fred Harvey imprint; a few are included that were issued by other publishers but reflect Fred Harvey-related images.

"Phostint" Printing

In the first decades of the twentieth century, most Harvey postcards were published by the Detroit Publishing Company (formerly the Detroit Photographic Company), using a registered photochrom printing process known as "Phostint." Originating in Switzerland, this process enabled the company to convert black-and-white photographs into color images and print them by photolithography. Phostint printing began in 1906 and continued until the early 1930s. The early Harvey cards are identified as either *Detroit Publishing Company Phostint* or *Fred Harvey Phostint* and a series of digits. The later Harvey cards include the Series H-1199 to H-4160 that were contract cards printed from 1901-1932 for Fred Harvey. After Harvey's contract with the Detroit Publishing Company ended in 1932, the Harvey Company continued to use the H-series through the Linen and Modern Photochrome postcard eras.

As with all collectibles, condition of the postcards can be rated from lesser to mint, although "mint" is seldom seen in vintage postcards. The condition contributes to pricing of individual postcards. Variables include discoloration, bends and creases, worn or rounded corners, writing or cancellation postmarks on the view side, along with other factors such as scarcity, regionalism, and associated levels of collecting interest. As a consequence, the values attributed to the postcards shown in this book are usually expressed as a value range.

○ Chapter 1
The Santa Fe Railway Goes Southwest

The railroad that became known as the Atchison Topeka and Santa Fe Railway in 1863 is universally known as "the Santa Fe." The Santa Fe's routes through the American Southwest, particularly New Mexico and Arizona, spawned interplay among the railroad, the Fred Harvey Company of restaurants and hotels, and the natural and cultural features of the region.

The Route Through New Mexico

After competing with other railroads for the right to build a viable route through this state, the Santa Fe entered New Mexico in November of 1878. After the right-of-way over Raton Pass at the Colorado-New Mexico border had been secured, a 2,000-foot tunnel through the summit of the pass was drilled at the elevation of 7,622 feet. This tunnel, initially a single track, was later widened to accommodate two tracks and provided generations of passengers entry to the "Great Southwest."

From the back: "Raton Tunnel, the highest point on the Santa Fe. Altitude 7,622 feet. The tunnel at Raton Pass is 15 miles beyond Trinidad, Colorado. The track follows the Old Santa Fe Trail, which is one of the oldest human pathways found on this continent." Pre-1930, Fred Harvey Phostint 10977; $3-5

From the back: "One of the incidents to be remembered on the transcontinental journey is the crossing of Raton Pass, between Trinidad, Colorado, and Raton, New Mexico. The train is drawn by two, and sometimes three engines, to the mouth of Raton Tunnel at the summit of the pass." Pre-1930, Phostint H-1561; $3-5

RATON TUNNELS-THE HIGHEST POINT ON THE SANTA FE-BETWEEN TRINIDAD, COLORADO AND RATON, NEW MEXICO.

H-1563 EVENING IN APACHE CANYON, BETWEEN LAS VEGAS AND LAMY, N. M.

From the back: "After leaving Las Vegas, the road winds over park slopes to the commanding height of Glorietta Pass (Alt. 7,422 ft.). The downward ride is thru Apache Canyon, where, in 1849 noted battles were fought between Kearney's army and the Mexicans, and in 1862 between Federal and Confederate forces." Pre-1930, Phostint H-1563; $6-8

Upon leaving the city of Raton at the southern base of the pass, the Santa Fe tracks ran through Las Vegas, New Mexico, passed 18 miles from New Mexico's capital city of Santa Fe at Lamy, and on to Albuquerque. Although displeased that the Santa Fe main line did not pass through their city, the citizens of Santa Fe assisted funding of a spur line from Lamy to the capital. Through construction and the acquisition of rights-of-way from other railroad companies, the Santa Fe completed the 750-mile route to Needles, California, at the Colorado River Bridge in 1883. In addition, the Santa Fe added other regional and cutoff lines in both New Mexico and Arizona.

By the early 1880s, the Santa Fe opened this region to passenger and freight rail traffic. In the coming years, the region's climate, scenery, culture, and history were insrumental in generating income for the railroad. The route that passed through world-class natural scenery and the rich cultural heritage of both Native American and Spanish cultures, the Santa Fe used a variety of approaches to promote the Southwest and generate ticket sales by including marketing of the region's natural and cultural virtues. As a business partner that handled most of the off-railroad ventures, the Fred Harvey Company thrived.

From the back: "Gliding through Apache Canyon near Lamy, New Mexico, is one of the most picturesque stretches along the Santa Fe Railway." Pre-1960, Fred Harvey C-5803; $3-5

8

A large number of disembarked Santa Fe passengers are shown in front of the Fred Harvey Indian Building at the Alvarado Hotel, Albuquerque, New Mexico. Pre-1930; $3-5

SCENE AT SANTA FE STATION, ALBUQUERQUE, NEW MEXICO

The Santa Fe Super Chief in front of the Albuquerque depot and Fred Harvey Alvarado Hotel, ready to continue its journey from Chicago to Los Angeles. Pre-1945; $4-6

From the back: "All fast Santa Fe Streamliners stop at Albuquerque, New Mexico's largest city. Located here are the famous (Fred Harvey) Alvarado Hotel and well-known Indian Building, where the finest Indian-made items may be secured by the many visitors of the great Southwest." Pre-1960; $4-6

The first single-track bridge at Canyon Diablo in eastern Arizona was completed in 1882 by the Atlantic and Pacific Railroad, a predecessor of the Santa Fe Railway. The bridge was replaced in 1900, and again in 1947 with a double-track, steel-arch bridge. Pre-1907, Detroit Publishing Company No. 5506; $3-5

5506. THE BRIDGE, CANYON DIABLO, ARIZONA

H-1574   SANTA FE TRAIN CROSSING JOHNSON'S CANYON, ARIZONA

A view of a Santa Fe passenger train crossing Johnson's Canyon and approaching the tunnel, west of Williams, Arizona. Pre-1945, H-1574; $3-5

From the back: "This new double track bridge is the third bridge the Santa Fe Railway has had across the Colorado River in the vicinity of Needles and at Topock. Its total length is 1506 feet." Pre-1945, H-4509; $2-3

H-4509—SANTA FE BRIDGE OVER COLORADO RIVER, NEAR TOPOCK, ARIZONA

10

From the back: "The Needles Mountains and Colorado River. Next to the Columbia, the Colorado River is the principal tributary to the Pacific. It was discovered in 1540 by Alarcon, who ascended at a considerable distance from the Gulf of California." Pre-1930, Fred Harvey No. 2662; $1-2

2662   THE NEEDLES, COLORADO RIVER, ARIZ.

An early Santa Fe passenger train is shown entering California from the Southwest, crossing the San Gabriel Valley under the shadow of the lofty Sierra Madre Range. Pre-1930, H-2290; $4-6

H-2290.   SANTA FE TRAIN ENTERING SOUTHERN CALIFORNIA THROUGH THE ORANGE GROVES.

H-5002   THE SUPER CHIEF—LUXURIOUS TRANSCONTINENTAL STREAMLINED FLYER

From the back: "The Super Chief – Santa Fe's all Pullman 39¾ - hour Chicago-Los Angeles flyer – with its nine cars, streamlined in gleaming, stainless steel, and 3600 H.P. Diesel-electric locomotive, weighs 709 tons. The locomotive, capable of 120 miles an hour and equipped with the latest safety devices, requires less effort to drive than an automobile." Pre-1945, H-5002; $6-8

From the back: "Fitted with roomy sofas, comfortable big chairs, and small tables facing a modernistic bar, the lounge car on the "Super Chief" has paneled walls of exquisite woods with inlaid Indian ceremonial figures, and authentic Navajo patterns in the window shades and decorations."
Pre-1945, H-4512; $8-10

H-4512—LOUNGE CAR ON THE SANTA FE'S "SUPER CHIEF"

H-4511—ONE OF THE FRED HARVEY DINING CARS ON THE SANTA FE'S "SUPER CHIEF"

From the back: "One of the unique features of the dining cars on the "Super Chief" is the specially designed china, featuring Indian designs found on the centuries-old pottery of New Mexico."
Pre-1945, H-4511; $8-10

H-4583—A SANTA FE STREAMLINED TRAIN

From the back: "Santa Fe Transcontinental Train – with its streamlined cars gleaming stainless steel and 6000 H.P. Diesel-electric locomotive." Pre-1945, H-4583; $4-6

The Hi-Level El Capitan passenger train passes through Shoemaker Canyon, New Mexico in the trip between Chicago and Los Angeles. Pre-1960, Fred Harvey C-5804; $3-4

From the back: "Designed to serve economy-minded coach fare travelers, the Santa Fe's El Capitan equals the time of the fastest deluxe trains between Chicago and Los Angeles." Pre-1960, Fred Harvey C-5806; $3-4

From the back: "Passengers relax leisurely for a luxurious Fred Harvey meal in the dining car of the Santa Fe's streamlined transcontinental El Capitan." Pre-1960, Fred Harvey C-5317; $4-6

The Santa Fe Railway and Native Americans

A significant part of the Santa Fe's marketing strategy was associating the railway with southwestern Native American themes. They called trains and individual sleeping and dining cars by Indian names and used tribal insignia as logos in their advertising materials. Many Native American designs appeared on their calendars and menus that were inspired by a famous Santa Fe Railway art collection that had been acquired in the 1880 to 1920 period. In addition, the Santa Fe employed Indian men as laborers along the route and as guides on the trains.

From the back: "Conrad Blue Wing, Harry War Bow, Lowell Sunrise from Zuni Pueblo of New Mexico. The Indian Guides on the Santa Fe Super Chief and El Capitan trough New Mexico." Pre-1960; $5-7

10947 FIRST SANTA FE TRAIN

From a painting by Frank P. Sauerwine, this Fred Harvey postcard image shows a group of Indians watching the first Santa Fe train crossing the continent, a harbinger of events to come for Southwestern Native Americans. Pre-1930, Fred Harvey Phostint 10947; $4-5

Conrad Blue Wing

Ralph Rolling Cloud

Lone Feather

Lowell Sun Rise

Indian Guides on the Santa Fe

From the back: "Indian Guides from Zuni Pueblo, New Mexico, ride the eastbound Santa Fe Super Chief and westbound El Capitan through New Mexico." Pre-1960; $5-7

The Santa Fe Railway's all-Indian Band is shown participating in the parade at the Gallup, New Mexico, Inter-Tribal Indian Ceremonial. Pre-1960; $3-4

An early Santa Fe passenger train is shown pausing at the Pueblo of Laguna, some 66 miles west of Albuquerque. Pre-1930, Fred Harvey Phostint 79084; $5-7

Pueblo Indian women selling pottery meet the Santa Fe transcontinental trains at the Pueblo of Laguna in New Mexico. Pre-1915, Detroit Publishing Company Phostint 6848; $7-9

Navajos watching games, the Fields, Arizona – On line of Santa Fe Railway. Pre-1915; $4-6

A Navajo poker game, Arizona – On the Santa Fe Railway. Pre-1915; $4-6

Hopi Indian dwelling, Arizona – On line of Santa Fe Railway. Pre-1915; $4-6

Williamson-Haffner
Postcards

Most of the postcards published and sold by the Santa Fe Railway and Fred Harvey Company were manufactured under contract to the Harvey Company. The Detroit Publishing Company provided Fred Harvey with postcards between 1901 and 1932. In 1907, the Williamson Haffner Company of Denver, Colorado (a business partner of the well-known H.H. Tammen Curio Company), produced a series of Native American images, each of which includes either the notation "On the Line of Santa Fe R.R.," or "On Santa Fe Ry." They appear to have been sold along the railway. Of those shown in the following images that were mailed, either postmarks are from stops along the route or are Santa Fe train Railway Post Office (RPO) stamps. The RPO was a railroad car that was normally operated on Santa Fe and other railroad passenger service to sort mail en-route and speed delivery.

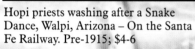

Hopi priests washing after a Snake
Dance, Walpi, Arizona – On the Santa
Fe Railway. Pre-1915; $4-6

Hopi Man weaving blanket, Oraibi,
Arizona – On the Santa Fe Railway.
Pre-1915; $4-6

White Mountain Apache girl,
Arizona – On line of Santa Fe
Railroad. Pre-1915; $4-6

A Hopi woman in wedding dress, Oraibi, Arizona – On Santa Fe Railway. Pre-1915; $4-6

616. A Hopi Woman in Wedding Dress, Oraibi, Ariz.
On Santa Fe Ry.

A White Mountain Apache "cupid," Arizona – On Santa Fe Railway. Pre-1915; $4-6

Hopi home life, Mishongnovi, Arizona – On Santa Fe Railroad. Pre-1915; $4-6

604. A White Mountain Apache "Cupid," Arizona.
On Santa Fe Ry.

618. Hopi Home Life, Mishongnoir, Arizona.—On Santa Fe Ry R.

White Mountain Apache hoops and javelin game, Arizona – On line of Santa Fe Railroad. Pre-1915; $4-6

Hopi moccasin makers, Oraibi, Arizona – On the Santa Fe Railway. Pre-1915; $4-6

Al-Che-Say, noted Apache Scout, White River Agency, Arizona – On line of Santa Fe Railway. Pre-1915; $6-8

Bonito, an Apache Scout, Fort Apache,
Arizona – On line of Santa Fe Railway.
Pre-1915; $6-8

Thomas Moran at Acoma Pueblo,
New Mexico – On line of Santa Fe
Railroad. Pre-1915; $12-14

Chapter 2

Fred Harvey in the Southwest, 1876-1901

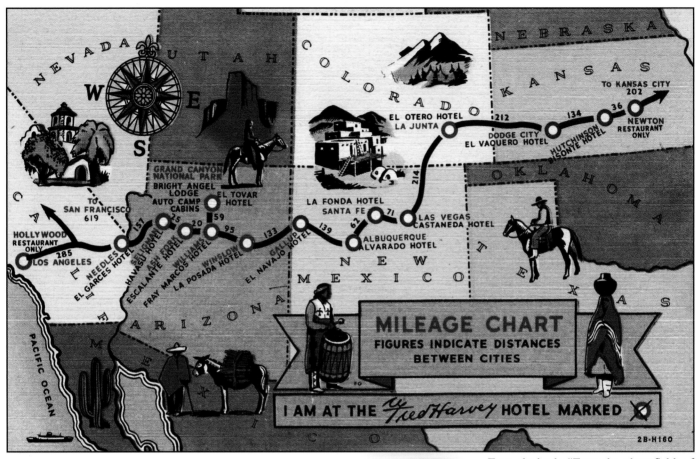

Along the Santa Fe Route

A business association between the Fred Harvey Company and the Santa Fe Railway began when Fred Harvey opened his first depot restaurant in Topeka, Kansas in January, 1876. Railroad officials and passengers alike were quickly impressed with Mr. Harvey's strict standards for high quality food and first class service. Harvey subsequently entered into contracts that enabled him to set up a series of restaurants, known as Harvey Houses, along the Santa Fe transcontinental route. Several of these eating-house locations evolved into hotels, especially in New Mexico and Arizona. By the late 1880s, there was a Fred Harvey dining facility located every 100 miles along the Santa Fe line.

While Fred Harvey establishments in Kansas, southeastern Colorado, and California were important to the overall system, the American Southwest was what the Fred Harvey Company and the Santa Fe Railway stressed in their marketing strategies. This region combined natural and cultural landscapes that could greatly benefit both companies.

From the back: "From the wheat fields of Kansas to the orange groves of California, the transcontinental highways which follow the popular 'Santa Fe Route' traverse a region rich in scenic interest... New Mexico with it mesas and pueblos, its ancient cliff dwellings and old Spanish missions...Arizona with its Grand Canyon, Painted Desert, Petrified Forest and colorful Indian Country. Along the way Fred Harvey Hotels provide convenient stops for meals and lodging and ideal headquarters for information concerning interesting journeys 'off the beaten path.'"
Pre-1945, H-4498; $6-8

The Natural Landscape

The American Southwest offered an unparalleled natural backdrop for the Santa Fe and Fred Harvey marketing strategies, and the mainline passenger route passed directly through or in proximity to some of the world's greatest geological wonders and scenic vistas. From the moment the westbound trains crossed Raton Pass, travelers were treated to endless views of landscapes dominated by mountains, plateaus, mesas, volcanic plugs and dikes, and canyons. Eroded geological features of nearly every shape and color added to nature's gallery.

H-1581 A GIANT CACTUS.

From the back: "The deserts of Arizona are not monotonous or lifeless – but are picturesque and beautiful. Plant life is not wanting. The Saguaro cactus is plentiful, towering to a height of 30 to 60 feet." Pre-1930, Phostint H-1581; $4-6

These eroded geological features near Gallup, New Mexico, are an example of the many scenic curiosities that enticed the Santa Fe's travelers to the Southwest. Pre-1930, H-2413; $2-3

H-2413 GEOLOGICAL FORMATIONS NEAR GALLUP, NEW MEXICO

Scenic La Bajada Hill, near the Santa Fe Route between Santa Fe and Albuquerque, New Mexico, offers a 1000-foot drop from the mesa to the valley below. Pre-1930; $2-3

LA BAJADA HILL, BETWEEN SANTA FE AND ALBUQUERQUE, NEW MEXICO 121023

H-3971 METEORITE CRATER NEAR WINSLOW, ARIZONA.

The spectacular Meteor Crater, located west of Winslow, Arizona, was a regular stop for Santa Fe passengers, and later travelers along the famous Route 66 Highway. Pre-1930, Phostint H-3971; $5-7

From the back: "The Painted Desert stretches for 300 miles along the north bank of the Little Colorado River. The most spectacular section of these vividly colored mesas, gullies, buttes, and ridges is part of Petrified Forest National Monument and a major point of interest to visitors of this famous area." Pre-1945, H-4550; $2-3

H-4550—THE PAINTED DESERT, ARIZONA 8B-H74

14933 THE PETRIFIED FOREST, ARIZONA.   COPR. FRED HARVEY

An example of Fred Harvey promotional writing is found on the back of this card–"From the remotest epochs earth has striven against seas in a struggle to free her face to air. Those who are learned may tell you where she is most deeply scarred by the conflict: in this region her triumph is complete, but her wounds are bare and with them many a secret she thought to lock forever in her bosom."
Pre-1930, Fred Harvey Phostint 14933; $2-4

From the back: "On the Navajo Reservation in northeastern Arizona are many canyons curiously carved out of the desert table lands. The most notable is a series some twenty miles long, called Canyon de Chelly, whose sheer narrow walls rise nearly a thousand feet." Pre-1945, H-2073; $2-3

H-2073 CANYON DE CHELLY, ARIZONA

Pre-1930, Phostint H-3624; $5-7

Pre-1930, Phostint H-3627; $5-7

25

The Grand Canyon

Starting with a baseline of endless scenic views of colorful geologic formations and eroded peaks, mesas, plateaus, and canyons, the Southwest contained a veritable landscape dream for eastern travelers used to forested areas with limited viewscapes or treeless and featureless plains. Without a doubt, the crown jewel of these natural settings was the Grand Canyon area of northern Arizona. The two companies were quick to capitalize on its natural wonder, as the railroad built a spur line from Williams, Arizona, to the canyon's south rim in 1901. In 1905, the Fred Harvey Company opened the grand El Tovar Hotel and later other tourist-related facilities.

Relying on the combination of historic Native American and Spanish cultures, along with the general magnetism of the "Wild West" concept, their strategy was to entice passengers to enjoy the Southwest and spend extra time and money doing so. The epitome of the region's cultural heritage was the area of North America's first capital city, Santa Fe, New Mexico. It had already lured travelers for several generations with its Pueblo-style architecture and deep-rooted Spanish traditions. Once brought to the town of Lamy, New Mexico, on the Santa Fe train, passengers were transported to the town of Santa Fe by motor vehicle where they experienced the unique cultural heritage and rich history of this picturesque city.

While staying at a Fred Harvey hotel, Santa Fe tourists were ferried by "Harveycars" to nearby Indian pueblos and small Hispanic villages where Southwestern culture, architecture, cuisine, and arts and crafts were experienced on a more intimate level. Once the "Indian-detour" trip was completed, tourists were placed back on the train to continue their journey that would include other Fred Harvey and Santa Fe stops and attractions in the Southwest.

From the back: "Looking north from El Tovar Hotel, showing Battleship Rock in the foreground and Isis Temple in the distance." Pre-1915, Hand-colored H-2377; $4-6

From the back: "General view from Bright Angel Cottage, Grand Canyon, Arizona." Pre-1915, Hand-colored H-2370; $4-6

View from the Watchtower, from
a painting by Gunnar Widforss.
Pre-1930, H-4488; $2-3

"AFTERNOON"—VIEW FROM THE WATCHTOWER, GRAND CANYON NATIONAL PARK, ARIZONA.   FROM PAINTING BY GUNNAR WIDFORSS.

COPR. FRED HARVEY.

79080 VIEW ON NORTH SIDE BELOW RAPID NO. 79, GRAND CANYON, ARIZ.

"MARICOPA POINT"—GRAND CANYON NATIONAL PARK, ARIZONA.
FROM PAINTING BY GUNNAR WIDFORSS.

Maricopa Point, from a painting by Gunnar
Widforss. Pre-1930, H-4479; $2-3

The Colorado River at the bottom of Grand
Canyon includes a series of perilous rapids.
Pre-1930, Fred Harvey Phostint 79080; $3-4

Pre-1930, Detroit Publishing Company Phostint 6322; $2-3

Pre-1915, Detroit Publishing Company
Phostint 7059; $3-4

The Grand Canyon of Arizona was the subject of several hundred Fred Harvey postcards
over the years. Pre-1930 Detroit Publishing Company Phostint 12295; $2-3

The Cultural Landscape

Just as the Southwest's natural setting offered considerable marketing potential to the Santa Fe's traveling public, the prehistoric and historic multicultural landscape included equal opportunities for enticing customers. Spectacular prehistoric aboriginal ruins, equally attractive ruins of relatively abandoned Spanish missions, and widespread continuity of both Native American and Hispanic cultures were abundant throughout the region, not to mention the spectacle of the more recent Euro-American "Wild West." Although Hispanic and Western cowboy images were employed in the promotion of New Mexico and Arizona, it was the Native American presence that was most exploited in Fred Harvey's Southwest.

H-2026 CLIFF KIVA, PUEBLO OF PU-YE, NEAR SANTA FE, NEW MEXICO.

Pre-1930, H-2026; $3-4

The prehistoric Pueblo of Puye is located near the modern-day Santa Clara Pueblo village, northeast of the town of Santa Fe, New Mexico. Pre-1930, H-35-07; $3-4

H-3507 PREHISTORIC CLIFF DWELLING, PUEBLO OF PUYE, NEAR SANTA FE, NEW MEXICO.

This early Fred Harvey postcard image shows ancient drawings on rock, located near Montezuma Castle National Monument, Camp Verde, Arizona. Pre-1915, Hand-colored, H-2268; $6-8

PICTOGRAPHS NEAR MONTEZUMA CASTLE, CAMP VERDE, ARIZONA.

H-3120   NAVAJO HORSEMEN IN CANYON DE CHELLY, ARIZONA.

Pre-1930, Phostint H-3120; $4-6

H-3511 PECOS PUEBLO (CICUYE) RUINS NEAR SANTA FE, NEW MEXICO.

From the back: "The ruins of Pecos Indian Mission church at the abandoned pueblo of Cicuye are thought by some to mark what was the greatest community center in America at the time of Columbus' discovery. Cicuye is supposed to have been continuously inhabited for 1200 years and here the Spaniards found the largest settlement in New Mexico." Pre-1930, Phostint, H-3511; $6-8

Another of the abandoned early Spanish Catholic churches in New Mexico was the La Quara Mission, located in the south-central part of the state. Pre-1930, H-1863; $3-4

H-1863 LAQUARA MISSION NEAR MOUNTAINAIR, N. MEX.

13925 OLD SPANISH CONVENT, LAMY, N. M   COPR. FRED HARVEY

From the back: "The town of Lamy, between Las Vegas and Albuquerque, was named for the good Archbishop who founded nearby a convent, the walls of which are still standing, and who also once taught Indians in a little adobe school house." Pre-1930, Fred Harvey Phostint 13925; $4-6

Pre-1915, Fred Harvey, Hand-colored, 519

The Old West was still very much alive in Fred Harvey's Southwest, as shown in these cattle branding images. Pre-1930, Fred Harvey Phostint 9239; $5-7

Pre-1930, Fred Harvey Phostint 8764; $5-7

From the back: "At Valley Ranch, on the upper Pecos River, 25 miles east of Santa Fe, is Apache Inn, providing every modern convenience for the traveler. Just a few miles down the river lie the ruins of the ancient Indian pueblo of Cicuye." Pre-1930, Phostint H-3515; $6-8

H-3515 APACHE INN, ON "THE INDIAN-DETOUR", BETWEEN LAS VEGAS AND SANTA FE, NEW MEXICO.

H-3522 THE OLDEST HOUSE IN AMERICA, SANTA FE, NEW MEXICO.

From the back: "The oldest house in Santa Fe stands across from the Chapel of San Miguel on the north side of De Vargas Street. This little 'dobe building is of Indian construction and is believed to antedate the permanent settlement of Santa Fe by Europeans in 1609." Pre-1930, Phostint H-3522; $4-5

From the back: "In the village of Fernandez de Taos is the old home of Kit Carson, famous scout, hunter, Indian fighter, and explorer who lived for many years in the country around Santa Fe." Pre-1930, Phostint H-3531; $3-5

H-3531 KIT CARSON'S HOUSE IN TAOS, NEW MEXICO.

34

From the back: "Santa Cruz is an ancient settlement to the north of Santa Fe on the road to Taos. Its mission church is said to be the most perfect in type in all of New Mexico." Pre-1930, Phostint H-3535; $6-8

H-3535 OLD MISSION CHURCH, SANTA CRUZ, NEW MEXICO.

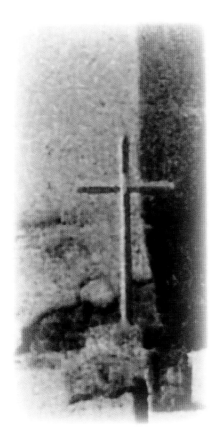

LAS VIGILES CHURCH, NEAR LAS VEGAS, NEW MEXICO.

A nice early Fred Harvey hand-colored image of the Spanish-American Las Vigiles church near Las Vegas, New Mexico. Pre-1915, Fred Harvey, Hand-colored No. 181; $14-16

H-3512 OLD INDIAN CHURCH, SAN JOSE, NEW MEXICO. 41.

From the back: "San Jose is a quaint Spanish-American settlement on the Santa Fe Trail between Las Vegas and Santa Fe. Here General Stephen E. Kearney, commanding the American Army, prepared for the decisive action against the Mexican forces which ended with the capture of Santa Fe in 1846." Pre-1930, Phostint H-3512; $6-8

The Pueblo of Taos, consisting of two multi-storied adobe communal houses, is the northernmost of the New Mexico Pueblo Indian villages. Located just north of the modern-day town of Taos, the pueblo is considered to be among the most picturesque of the pueblos. Pre-1930, Phostint H-3539; $3-5

From the back: "Laguna (the Lake) was founded in 1699 and is the youngest of the pueblos. It is 66 miles west of Albuquerque, New Mexico." Pre-1915, Detroit Publishing Company Photostint 11596: $5-7

The Pueblo of San Felipe lies on the east bank of the Rio Grande River, about 30 miles north of Albuquerque, New Mexico. The mission church, seen at the right part of the image, has two towers and a large yard, the whole being enclosed with a high arched adobe wall. Pre-1930, Phostint H-2235; $3-5

5509. PUEBLO OF ACOMA AND MESA ESCANTADA, N. M.   COPYRIGHT, 1899, BY DETROIT PHOTOGRAPHIC CO.

The Pueblo of Acoma, located in west-central New Mexico, is defensively situated atop a small sandstone mesa. The small picturesque mesa known as Mesa Encantada, can be seen in the background. Pre-1907, Detroit Publishing Company, No. 5509; $6-8

H-3965   ORAIBI, A HOPI INDIAN VILLAGE, ARIZONA.

This postcard image and the one at the top of the next page are of Oraibi, located in northeastern Arizona. Oraibi, one of the oldest of the Hopi villages, is also one of the oldest continuously inhabited communities in North America. Pre-1930, Phostint H-3965; $6-8

The Hopi Pueblo of Oraibi, Arizona, showing two important ceremonial Kivas or Chambers in foreground.

Pre-1915, Fred Harvey, unnumbered; $10-12.

13911 NAVAHO INDIAN FAMILY AND HOGAN, ARIZONA. COPR. FRED HARVEY.

From the back: "The Navajo Indian Reservation is reached from Gallup, Holbrook, and Winslow. These Indians are called Bedouins of the desert from the fact that they never settle for any length of time in one village, but live in hogans or temporary structures and travel from place to place. The Navajos are noted for their blankets, and they are also expert silversmiths. They are great horsemen and on the reservation raise numbers of sheep and goats." Pre-1930, Fred Harvey Phostint 13911; $4-5

13910 JEMEZ CHURCH, PUEBLO OF JEMEZ, N. M.   FRED HARVEY.

From the back: "There are some twenty inhabited Pueblo villages in New Mexico, comprising five tribal language stocks. Each Pueblo has its saint's day which is observed with the usual ceremonials. At Jemez this date is August 15th." Pre-1930, Fred Harvey Phostint 13910; $5-7

An early view of the Catholic mission church at the Pueblo of Isleta, located south of Albuquerque. The structure has been significantly remodeled over the decades and looks markedly different today. Pre-1915, Detroit Publishing Company, No. 6316; $6-8

6316. OLD CHURCH AT PUEBLO OF ISLETA, N. M.   FROM PHOTO COPYRIGHT 1902, BY DETROIT PHOTOGRAPHIC CO.

COPR. FRED HARVEY.

79014 APACHE WAR PARTY, ARIZONA. ON THE SANTA FE.

AFTER PAINTING BY CHARLES CRAIG.

From the back: "The Havasupais are allied with the Walapai, their neighbor on the west, and speak the same language with slight variations of dialect. Their village is romantically situated in Cataract Canyon, some fifty miles west of Grand Canyon and about one hundred miles from Williams, Arizona. The Havasupai woman has the distinction of being the only one to cook meats and mush in coiled willow trays."

Above: Pre-1930, Fred Harvey Photostint 79014; $5-7.
Below Left: Pre-1930, Fred Harvey Phostint 10982; $7-9

Below: In the Southwest of Fred Harvey and the Santa Fe Railway, the Apaches were still remembered for the well-documented Apache Wars of the 1880s. By 1900, the Apaches were located on widely separated reservations – the Jicarilla and Mescalero in New Mexico, and the San Carlos and White Mountain in Arizona. Fred Harvey Phostint 13940; $3-5

10982 HAVASUPAI WOMAN WITH CARRYING BASKET AT CATARACT CANYON, ARIZONA. FRED HARVEY.

13940 IN APACHE LAND, ARIZONA. COPR. FRED HARVEY.

Harvey Company Hotels and Facilities, 1901-1960s

Fred Harvey, an entrepreneur who in 1876 began his hospitality empire of Harvey House lunchrooms, restaurants, souvenir shops, and hotels, died in 1901. The founder left the Fred Harvey Company to his sons and grandsons to run, and it prospered until the late 1960s. At the time of his death, there were 47 Harvey House restaurants, 15 hotels, and 30 dining cars operating on the Santa Fe Railway. Eleven years after Fred Harvey's death, the chain included more than 65 eating houses, 12 hotels, and 60 dining cars. In the late 1940s, the Harvey system operated about 50 restaurants, a dozen major hotels, 100 newsstands, several dozen retail shops, and supervised service on over 100 dining cars. Of the 23 major hotels operated by the Harvey Company over the years, 14 of these were located in New Mexico and Arizona, with many being named after early Spanish conquistadores and explorers.

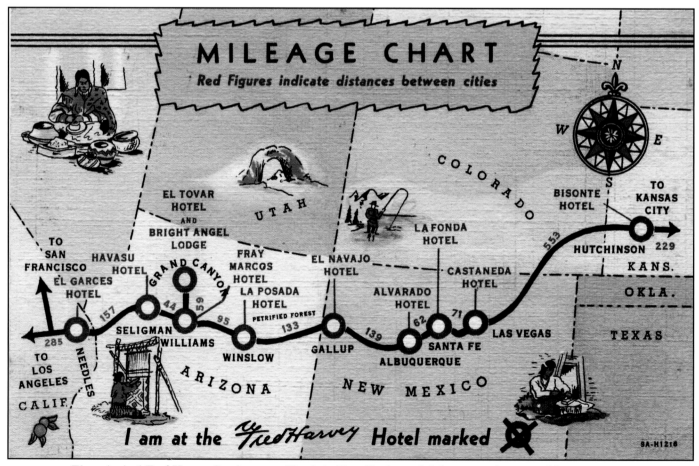

The principal Fred Harvey Southwestern Hotels in New Mexico and Arizona are shown on this map postcard. Train passengers were offered a handy way to indicate their current location to those at home. Pre-1945, H-4479; $6-8

41

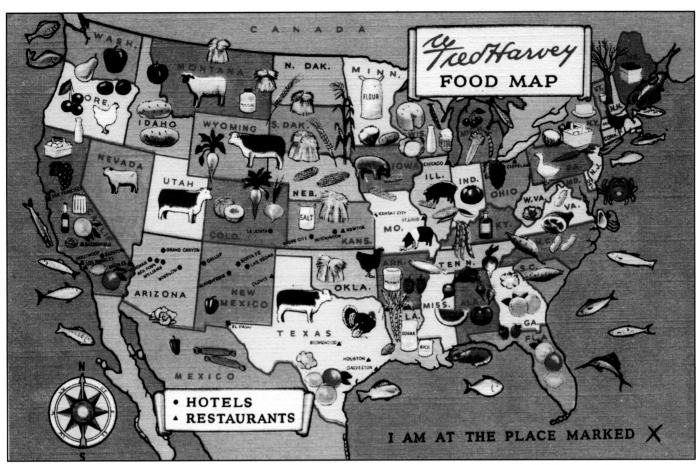

With the aid of the Santa Fe's ice cars, Fred Harvey was able to bring fresh meat, produce, and milk to all eating houses and hotel dining rooms along the route. Good water was even brought to towns to ensure that Harvey's special blend of coffee was not spoiled by local water that had an alkali taste. Pre-1945, H-4506; $6-8

In the years between 1900 and World War I, the American Southwest became a favorite of upper-class Americans and Europeans who sought adventurous excursions and leisurely vacations. Fred Harvey and Santa Fe Railway were quick to appreciate the potential of this booming interest in the region. Thus, the companies began expanding their services to attract the new stopover passenger traffic, especially by building luxurious hotels and extensive facilities to provide railroad travelers with resort-like accommodations along the rail line. In the Southwest, the Fred Harvey Company hired architect Mary Colter to give many of these new buildings special and local touches, particularly in the use of Native American and Spanish design and architectural elements.

As had been the case since the inception of Fred Harvey lunchroom service in the 1870s, high standards for efficiency and cleanliness were the hallmarks of the Southwestern Harvey hotels. Hotel dining rooms included tableside service by the famed "Harvey Girls." This company tradition went back to 1893 when Fred Harvey hired respectable young women, recruited from the Midwest and the East as waitresses to serve his customers. For the young women assigned to work at the grand hotels along the Santa Fe, it was a great privilege to live in beautiful and unusual places such as the Grand Canyon, the old plaza in Santa Fe, and the ancient Native American areas around Gallup, New Mexico, and Winslow, Arizona.

Owing to national events such as the depression years and modernization of passenger travel, Harvey facilities began a gradual decline that would culminate by the 1960s with the closing of nearly all the hotels. A brief revival associated with intensive movement of troops during World War II saw entire Santa Fe trains and Harvey hotels filled with military passengers. The Fred Harvey Company itself was finally bought out in 1968. Today, only three of the original Southwestern Harvey hotels have remained in continuous operation: the La Fonda on the plaza in Santa Fe, and the Bright Angel Lodge and El Tovar Hotel at Grand Canyon National Park. A fourth, the La Posada Hotel in Winslow, Arizona, was reopened in the late 1990s after having been closed in 1957.

Pre-1915, Fred Harvey, unnumbered; $8-10

Pre-1915, Fred Harvey, unnumbered; $10-12

The Cardenas

In Trinidad, Colorado, the Cardenas Hotel was built in 1903 as a two-story, L-shaped, Mission Style building with a red-tiled roof and arcaded porch. It was the last Harvey-operated hotel along the Santa Fe route before entering New Mexico. The Cardenas was closed and razed in 1933.

From the back: "Raton, which is almost exactly midway between Chicago and Los Angeles, is an important center of the cattle industry and is located on the line of inexhaustible coal deposits. Raton is the site of extensive railroad machine shops and the headquarters of the Maxwell Land Grant Company." Pre-1915, Fred Harvey Phostint 10991

The Castaneda

Las Vegas, New Mexico, population 10,000, altitude 6401 feet. Located on Railroad Avenue, one block off Highway 85.

Rates from $1.50 without bath and $2.50 with bath—European plan. Coffee Shop and Dining Room service available at reasonable prices. Cocktail Service, News Stand.

Las Vegas is the gateway to the New Mexico Mountain Country. Good fishing and hunting. (From a 1941 Fred Harvey Company brochure)

The Montezuma Hotel, located about six miles from the town of Las Vegas, New Mexico, was the Santa Fe and Fred Harvey's first hotel venture in the Southwest. The resort hotel opened in 1882 to take advantage of local hot springs. The hotel burned down twice and was rebuilt each time before 1899. It was finally closed by the Santa Fe in 1903, being replaced by the new Castaneda Hotel, located in town and on the tracks. Pre-1915, Fred Harvey, unnumbered; $8-10

Pre-1915, Detroit Publishing Company Phostint 13991; $6-8

Pre-1915, Fred Harvey Phostint 14907; $10-12

Pre-1915, Fred Harvey Phostint 10962; $6-8

44

El Ortiz

In New Mexico, about 18 miles southeast of Santa Fe, the small town of Lamy began in 1880 as a railroad junction between the Santa Fe's main east-west line and the capital city of Santa Fe. The El Ortiz was built in 1910, replacing a wooden depot hotel that had burned. The hotel closed in 1938 and was razed in 1943. Designing the interior of the new El Ortiz was architect Mary Colter's first job for the Fred Harvey Company.

Pre-1915, Fred Harvey Phostint 79031; $6-8

Pre-1915, Fred Harvey Phostint 79025; $8-10

Pre-1915, Fred Harvey Phostint 79027; $8-10

79087 THE LOBBY, HOTEL EL ORTIZ, LAMY, N. M.   FRED HARVEY.

Pre-1915, Fred Harvey Phostint 79087; $8-10

79026 MANTLE PIECE IN LOBBY, EL ORTIZ HOTEL, LAMY, NEW MEXICO.   FRED HARVEY.

Pre-1915, Fred Harvey Phostint 79026; $8-10

79024 THE PLACITA, EL ORTIZ HOTEL, LAMY, NEW MEXICO

Pre-1915, Fred Harvey Phostint 79024; $8-10

46

La Fonda

Located in the center of Santa Fe, New Mexico, population 20,000, altitude 6969 feet, the La Fonda hotel was "The Inn at the end of the [Santa Fe] trail," on the town's main plaza where highways 64, 84, 85, and 285 meet.

Rates originally were from $2 without bath and $3 with bath on the European plan. Living room suites were from $13.50. Special rates for extended occupancy. Table d'hote and a la carte service at reasonable prices. Delicious Mexican food was a feature.

Sunny Patio, Old World Charm, Orchestra from Old Mexico, Dinner Dancing, Music at Teat Time, Cantina (Cocktail Room), La Placita (outdoor dining), News Stand, Indian and Mexican Curio Store, Barber Shop, Beauty Shop, Sample Rooms. Informal Entertainments, Horseback Riding, Golf, Trout Fishing, Skiing, Colorful Fiestas. Annual Santa Fe Fiesta usually held in the first week in September. La Fonda serves as delightful headquarters for daily trips to Indian Pueblos, cliff dwellings, prehistoric ruins, primitive Mexican villages. Headquarters for Indian-detour. Cool summers. Mild winters.

Santa Fe is the oldest capital in the United States and is in the center of the most interesting hundred mile square in America.
(From a 1941 Fred Harvey Company brochure)

Pre-1945; $4-6

Pre-1930, Phostint H-3951; $6-8

Pre-1945; $4-6

Pre-1930, Phostint H-3502; $6-8

H-3502   LA FONDA HOTEL, SANTA FE, NEW MEXICO.

The Alvarado

Located in Albuquerque, New Mexico. Population 50,000, Altitude 4953 feet, at the crossing of First Street and Central Avenue, Highways 66 and 85.

Rates from $1.50 without bath and $2.50 with bath – European plan. Table d'hotel and a la carte meal service at reasonable prices.

Coffee Shop, Dining Room, Private Dining Room, La Cocina Cantina (Cocktail Room), La Placita (outdoor dining), News Stand, Sample Rooms, Barber Shop, Beauty Shop. Rambling Spanish Mission type of architecture with wide verandas and inviting patios. Adjoining the hotel is the Fred Harvey Indian building with its world famous exhibits of Indian and Mexican crafts. Indians weaving in the curio shop. Several Indian pueblos within a few miles. Albuquerque is the largest city in the State of New Mexico. There is an all-grass eighteen hole Country Club golf course available to the guests of The Alvarado. Old Plaza, Spanish Mission Church of San Filipe de Neri, erected about 1735. (From a 1941 Fred Harvey Company brochure)

Pre-1930, Phostint H-2895; $5-7

Pre-1915, Fred Harvey Phostint 5994; $5-7

From the back: "In the northern New Mexico Rockies lies the Enchanted Empire of the Southwest. Its center is Santa Fe. The Taos of Kit Carson is on its northern edge. Las Vegas and Albuquerque are along the eastern and southern boundaries. This Enchanted Empire may now be visited comfortable and at reasonable cost via the new "Indian-detour" – a three day personally-conducted motor trip forming part of the transcontinental journey over the Santa Fe railroad." Pre-1930, Phostint H-3541; $14-16

48

Pre-1960, Real photo; $14-16

Pre-1945, H-4476; $4-6

ALBUQUERQUE, NEW MEXICO
Pueblo Indians at the train

Pre-1915; $ 6-8

Pre-1930, Phostint H-1927; $5-7

Pre-1945, H-4475; $4-6

Pre-1915, Fred Harvey Phostint 12951; $10-12

50

H-1929. INDIAN WORK ROOM, THE INDIAN BUILDING, ALBUQUERQUE, NEW MEXICO

From the back: "In the Indian Building at Albuquerque are a number of Navajos spinning and dying wool, weaving blankets, and making silver ornaments with their crude tools." Pre-1930, H-1929; $3-5

H-1928. MANTEL PIECE, THE INDIAN BUILDING, ALBUQUERQUE, NEW MEXICO

Pre-1930, H-1928; $5-7

7945. A GROUP OF NAVAHOS, ALBUQUERQUE, N. M.   COPYRIGHT, 1905, BY FRED HARVEY.

A group of Navajos at the Indian Room, Alvarado Hotel, in 1907, including the famous weaver Elle of Ganado, third from left, and her husband Tom to her right. Pre-1907, Fred Harvey 7945; $4-6

An old Navajo Bayetta style blanket, from the Fred Harvey Blanket collection,
Indian Room, Albuquerque, New Mexico. Pre-1907, Fred Harvey 7941; $6-8

52

H-1925. NAVAHO SILVERSMITH. INDIAN BUILDING.

ALBUQUERQUE, NEW MEXICO.

H-2012 A PRIMITIVE INDIAN VILLAGE IN THE HEART OF A MODERN CITY, ALBUQUERQUE, NEW MEXICO.

A replica pueblo structure was built by the Indians working in the Indian Building at Albuquerque so that they could live as in their home villages. Pre-1930, Phostint H-2012; $6-8

Pre-1930, H-1925; $4-6

Indian Hogan, Albuquerque, N.M.

Similar to the Pueblo peoples working at the Indian Building in Albuquerque, the Navajos preferred their traditional dwelling. This hogan, constructed in downtown Albuquerque housed Elle of Ganado and her family in the early 1900s. Pre-1915, Hand-colored; $10-12

53

H-1926—INTERIOR OF FRED HARVEY INDIAN BUILDING, ALBUQUERQUE, NEW MEXICO

Pre-1945, H-1926; $4-6

H-1932.   A CORNER IN THE SPANISH ROOM, THE INDIAN BUILDING, ALBUQUERQUE, NEW MEXICO

Pre-1930, H-1932; $5-7

H-4543—FIREPLACE IN THE FRED HARVEY INDIAN BUILDING, ALBUQUERQUE, NEW MEXICO

Pre-1945, H-4543; $4-6

54

The Fred Harvey Alvarado Hotel outlasted many of Southwestern railroad hotels, remaining open until 1968. These three postcards from the late 1950s show the hotel in its later days, including the longstanding tradition of Indians selling their crafts in front of the Indian Building. The structure was razed in 1970 with many former Harvey employees and railroad people looking on.

Pre-1960; $3-5

Pre-1960; $3-5

Pre-1960; $3-5

90184 GRAN QUIVIRA AND SANTA FE STATION, CLOVIS, N. M.

Pre-1930, Fred Harvey 90184; $6-8

Gran Quivira

Located in Clovis, New Mexico, on the Belen Cutoff line between Amarillo, Texas, and the railroad's mainline through New Mexico. The Gran Quivira was built by the Santa Fe Railway about 1900, as a reinforced concrete hotel patterned after early California Spanish missions. The hotel closed in the 1940s.

H-3572   Gran Quivira, Santa Fe Hotel, Clovis, New Mexico.

Pre-1930, H-3572; $8-10

H-4112   Santa Fe Hospital   Clovis, New Mexico

In addition to the hotels and eating houses managed by Fred Harvey, the Santa Fe constructed reading rooms and hospitals along the route for its employees. The Santa Fe Hospital in Clovis, New Mexico, was built in 1914 and had a capacity of 50 patients. Pre-1930, H-4112; $6-8

H-3563   Santa Fe Eating House   Vaughn, New Mexico

The Harvey House and a small hotel known as the "Las Chavez" opened in Vaughn, New Mexico, about 1910. The hotel closed in 1936. Pre-1930, H-3563; $8-10

H-1393 NEW SANTA FE HOTEL, BELEN, NEW MEXICO.

The Belen, New Mexico, Harvey House operated between 1907 and 1935. Today, the building still stands and holds a Harvey House museum. Pre-1930, H-1393; $6-8

El Navajo

Located in Gallup, New Mexico. Population 6,700, altitude 6505 feet. Highways 66 and 666 cross here.

Rates from $1.50 without bath and $2.50 with bath – European plan. Table d'hotel and a la carte meal service at reasonable prices.

Coffee Shop, Dining Room, Cocktail Lounge, News Stand.

Spanish and Indian architecture. Colorful Navajo sand-paintings adorn the walls of the public rooms. Headquarters for many very interesting trips into the Indian Country – Zunis and Navajos. Acoma and Enchanted Mesa 105 miles. Painted Desert, Ice Caves, Inscription Rock, and Petrified Forest accessible from here. Chaco Canyon 95 miles. Annual Inter-Tribal Indian Ceremonial usually around the middle of August. Gateway to the Snake Dance. Extensive coal mining district. Station of old pony express. (From a 1941 Fred Harvey Company brochure)

H-1892 EL NAVAJO, FRED HARVEY HOTEL, GALLUP, NEW MEXICO.   (AFTER PAINTING BY FRED GEARY)

Pre-1930, H-1892; $5-7

H-3142   THE LOBBY, EL NAVAJO HOTEL, GALLUP, NEW MEXICO

99475

Pre-1930, H-3142; $10-12

The Painted Desert Inn in the Petrified Forest National Monument in northeastern Arizona opened for business in 1940. In 1947 it was taken over by the Fred Harvey Company who operated it until 1963. Since closing as an inn and restaurant, the building has been used intermittently as a museum, interpretive space, and meeting hall by the National Park Service. Pre-1945, H-4548; $6-8

4548— THE PAINTED DESERT INN, PETRIFIED FOREST NATIONAL MONUMENT, ARIZONA

8B-H72

La Posada

Located in Winslow, Arizona, population 5,500 , altitude 4856 feet. East Second Street at Highways 65 and 66.

Rates from $1.50 without bath and $2.50 with bath—European plan. Living room suites from $10.00. Table d'hote and a la carte meal service at reasonable prices.

Coffee Shop, Restaurant, Private Dining Room, Cocktail Service, News Stand.

With its Spanish architecture and its delightful gardens, a refreshing oasis in the colorful mesa land of Northern Arizona. Delightful headquarters for motor trips into the surrounding Navajo and Hopi Indian country. Meteor Crater, Painted Desert, Petrified Forest, Canyon Diablo, Canyon de Chelly, Tonto Rim and Basin Country easily reached from here. (From a 1941 Fred Harvey Company brochure)

Prior to the opening of the La Posada Hotel in Winslow, Arizona, an earlier Fred Harvey Hotel operated across the tracks from the later establishment. Like other Harvey hotels of the time, it had guest rooms, a dining room, and a lunchroom; unlike other hotels, it does not appear to have been named.
Pre-1930, Phostint H-2873; $6-8

Pre-1930, H-3979; $6-8

60

60

Pre-1945, H-4224; $5-7

H-4224 LA POSADA, FRED HARVEY HOTEL, WINSLOW, ARIZONA

H-4157 PASSAGEWAY TO WEST WING, LA POSADA, FRED HARVEY HOTEL, WINSLOW, ARIZONA

Pre-1945, H-4157; $5-7

H-4158 DINING ROOM, LA POSADA, FRED HARVEY HOTEL, WINSLOW, ARIZONA

Pre-1945, H-4158; $6-8

Santa Fe Eating House and Red Cross Canteen Hut,
Williams, Arizona.

Fray Marcos

Located in Williams, Arizona, population 2,000, altitude 6762 feet. At the crossing of Highways 66 and 89.

Rates from $1.50 without bath and $2.50 with bath—European plan. Table d'hote and a la carte meal service at reasonable prices.

Coffee Shop, Private Dining Rooms, News Stand.

With its surrounding mountain peaks and picturesque canyons, the town of Williams offers many attractions for motor tours. Gateway to Grand Canyon National Park. (From a 1941 Fred Harvey Company brochure)

Pre-1915; $10-12

11963 FRAY MARCOS, NEW SANTA FE HOTEL, WILLIAMS, ARIZONA. COPR. FRED HARVEY.

Pre-1915, Fred Harvey Phostint 11963; $6-8

12928 THE LOBBY, FRAY MARCOS, WILLIAMS, ARIZ. FRED HARVEY

Pre-1915, Fred Harvey Phostint 12928; $8-10

The Escalante, Ash Fork, Ariz.

COPYRIGHT 1907 BY FRED HARVEY

Pre-1915, Fred Harvey, unnumbered; $8-10

The Escalante

Located at Ash Fork, Arizona, population 1,000, altitude 5143 feet, at the crossing of Highways 66, 89.

Rates from $1.50 without bath and $2.50 with bath – European plan. Table d'hote and a la carte meal service at reasonable prices. Coffee Shop and Dining Room Service, News Stand. Ash Fork is a stock raising center, located on the northwest edge of the great Coconino Forest. Interesting Cathedral Caves 16 miles north. (From a 1941 Fred Harvey Company brochure)

H-3191   SELIGMAN, ARIZONA, SANTA FE STATION AND HOTEL IN FOREGROUND

Pre-1930, H-3191; $12-14

The Havasu

Located in Seligman, Arizona, population 600, altitude 5242 feet, at Highway 66.

Rates from $1.50 with bath and $2.50 with bath—European plan. Table d'hote and a la carte meal service at reasonable prices. Coffee Shop, News and Curio Stand.

Havasu Canyon, 70 miles to the north of Seligman, is a tributary of the Grand Canyon and home of the Havasupai Indians.

The Havasu is one of the few remaining Harvey Hotels that has been preserved in the original form. Meeting place of rangers, cowboys, freight conductors, motor and rail tourists. Interesting cattle ranches nearby. Excellent deer hunting. (From a 1941 Fred Harvey Company brochure)

H-2465.   THE SANTA FE LIMITED AT NEEDLES, CALIFORNIA.

Pre-1930, H-2465; $8-10

El Garces Hotel and Park. Needles, Cal.

Pre-1930, Fred Harvey, Hand-colored H-1784; $6-8

Santa Fe Shop Park.   Needles, Cal.

Pre-1930, Fred Harvey, Hand-colored H-1779; $6-8

El Garces

Located in Needles, California, population 4000, altitude 483 feet, on Highways 66 and 195.

Rates from $1.50 without bath and $2.50 with bath—European plan. Coffee Shop, Air Cooled, News Stand. Boulder Dam, Parker Dam, Mitchell Caverns, and Mojave Indian Reservation easily reached from here. Mojave Indians inhabit single room houses constructed of adobe and cross twigs in close proximity to the hotel. The Colorado River and Lake Havasu are within a short distance of the hotel and there are provisions for swimming, boating and fishing. Excellent bass, blue gill, perch, crappie and channel cat fishing.

El Garces is situated in one of the most beautiful parts of the desert country. Air-conditioning throughout, however, insures comfort at all times. (From a 1941 Fred Harvey Company brochure)

○ Chapter 4
The Grand Canyon Experience

At The Canyon

A massive subsequent publicity campaign was undertaken jointly by the Santa Fe and Fred Harvey companies that greatly increased public awareness of this "Titan of the Chasms." Their efforts undoubtedly played a part in establishing The Grand Canyon as a national park in 1919. Moreover, the canyon's splendor and heavy visitation certainly contributed significantly to postcard sales for the Fred Harvey Company.

At the Grand Canyon, as elsewhere along the rail line, arrangements between the Santa Fe and Fred Harvey Companies were atypical, but worked well at the time. Harvey operated the restaurants and hotels but owned only the furnishings. The buildings and land were owned by the Santa Fe Company. The only building at the Grand Canyon operated directly by the Santa Fe was a rustic log depot constructed in 1909.

The Santa Fe Railway and Fred Harvey recognized the potential for tourism that the Grand Canyon provided, but Fred Harvey himself would not live to see the outcome of his planning. The Grand Canyon was first reached by a branch line of the Santa Fe in 1901, extending 65 miles north from the main rail line at Williams, Arizona.

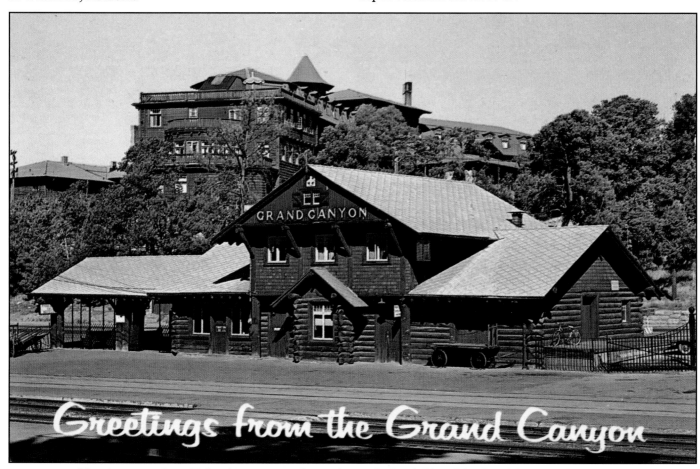

The picturesque Santa Fe log depot greets train travelers to the South Rim of the Grand Canyon. The majestic El Tovar Hotel looms in the background. Pre-1960, FH-201; $4-6

The El Tovar Hotel

The 100-room luxury El Tovar Hotel was completed in 1905 by the Fred Harvey Company and Santa Fe Railway within walking distance from the train terminus.

Located at The Grand Canyon, Arizona, on the South Rim, altitude 7000 feet near Highways 64, 66, and 89.

Rates from $2.50 without bath and $3.50 with bath— European plan. Rates from $5.50 without bath and $6.50 with bath—American plan. Table d'hote and a la carte meal service at reasonable prices.

Dining Room, News Stand, Southwestern Curio Store, Art Room, Cocktail Lounge. Excellent Garage.

One of the most famous resort inns in the world, picturesquely situated on the south rim of the Grand Canyon. The building, three stories high, of pine slabs fits the forest around it. El Tovar's rustic dining room is internationally renowned for its excellent cuisine. The hotel is the starting point for numerous motor and trail trips. Famous Grand Canyon Rim Drive to Hermit's Rest and The Watchtower at Desert View Point; picturesque Navahopi Road to Painted Desert, Navajo and Hopi Indian Reservation; bridle paths along the Rim; trail trips on muleback into the depths of the great chasm, to famous "down deep" Phantom Ranch across the Colorado River, and on to the North Rim.

The Grand Canyon, discovered 1540 by Spanish Explorers, is 217 miles long, 4 to 18 miles wide, a mile deep. Many evidences of ancient and present Indian life. The Hopi House, a replica of a Hopi Indian home, faces El Tovar. Members of the Hopi tribe live and work here. Indian Dances. (From a 1941 Fred Harvey Company brochure)

GRAND CANYON NATIONAL PARK, ARIZONA

H-3970 AIRPLANE VIEW OF GRAND CANYON (EL TOVAR HOTEL IN THE FOREGROUND)

Pre-1930, H-3970; $4-6

H-1538 HOTEL EL TOVAR, GRAND CANYON NATIONAL PARK, ARIZONA.   COPR. FRED HARVEY

Pre-1930, Phostint H-1538; $3-4

H-1510 HOTEL EL TOVAR, GRAND CANYON NATIONAL PARK, ARIZONA.

Pre-1930, Phostint H-1510; $4-6

The Start from El Tovar, Grand Canyon, Arizona.
COPYRIGHT 1907 BY FRED HARVEY

Pre-1915, Fred Harvey, unnumbered; $10-12

67

Pre-1930, Phostint H-1934; $5-7

Pre-1930, Phostint H-1924; $6-8

Pre-1915, Fred Harvey 9923; $$6-8

Architect Mary Colter

When El Tovar was completed and open for business, the Fred Harvey Company turned to its newly-hired architect, Mary Elizabeth Jane Colter, to design and oversee construction of a series of buildings at the Grand Canyon. They are still enjoyed today by millions of visitors annually. Colter designed Bright Angel Lodge, Hopi House, Hermit's Rest, the Lookout Studio, and the Desert View Watchtower, all constructed between 1905 and 1932. Colter's "parkarchitecture" is renowned today for its particular aesthetic and relationship to local Native American and natural landscapes and use of natural materials in forms that mimick nature.

Hermit Camp and Phantom Ranch

An early adjunct to tourism at the Grand Canyon involved enhancing the visitor's overall experience with tours along the rim and into the canyon. Initially tours were conducted by horseback at the rim trails and by mule into the canyon. Later, as the Fred Harvey Company and Santa Fe Railroad expanded the rim rail system, automobile and bus tours replaced the saddlehorse trips. Mule trips to the bottom of the canyon were supplemented by the construction of Hermit Camp part way down in 1912. It had a central dining hall and eleven tents, with accommodations for thirty people. In 1922, the more permanent Phantom Ranch, also designed by Mary Colter, was built at the canyon bottom to house overnight visitors.

The Santa Fe railroad ended regular passenger service to the Grand Canyon in 1968. That year the Amfac Corporation of Hawaii purchased the original Fred Harvey Company, including the Grand Canyon concession operations. In recent years, a privately owned Grand Canyon Railroad resumed service to the park and visitors can once again experience the nostalgic train ride from Williams to the Grand Canyon Depot.

Bright Angel Lodge

Located at the Grand Canyon, Arizona, on the South Rim, altitude 7000 feet.

Rooms in lodges and cabins from $2.00 without bath and $3.00 with bath—European plan. Auto camp facilities adjacent to public camp area $1.25 and up per cabin. Table d'hote and a la carte meal service at reasonable prices.

Coffee Shop, Restaurant, Cocktail Service, News Stand, Barber Shop, Beauty Shop.

The Bright Angel Lodge is just a stone's throw from El Tovar. These new facilities provide a wide range in comfortable, modern living accommodations in attractive lodges and in numerous individual cabins. The rambling one-story structures form a picturesque group on the Canyon's very rim—a little village of log, stone and adobe. In the rustic, informal lounge, huge windows reveal magnificent and unusual Grand Canyon vistas. All trips and entertainment from and at El Tovar are available to guests at the Bright Angel Lodge. Evening entertainment free. Cowboys, moving pictures, and dancing. Excellent garage facilities. Free parking space. (From a 1941 Fred Harvey Company brochure)

H-2768. BRIGHT ANGEL CAMP, GRAND CANYON NATIONAL PARK, ARIZONA.

The Bright Angel Camp was an early complex of cabins and tents beside a simple hotel structure, some elements of which pre-dated the arrival of the Santa Fe and Fred Harvey at the Grand Canyon. Taken over by Fred Harvey about 1907, the facility was eventually replaced by the Bright Angel Lodge, completed in 1935. Pre-1930, H-2768; $6-8

The rambling, one-story structures of Bright Angel Lodge and Cabins form a picturesque group on the Grand Canyon's rim. Pre-1945, H-4456; $3-5

H.4471 ENTRANCE TO BRIGHT ANGEL LODGE, GRAND CANYON NATIONAL PARK, ARIZONA

Pre-1945, H-4471; $3-5

Pre-1945, H-44-72; $3-5

H-4459   A CORNER IN THE LOUNGE, BRIGHT ANGEL LODGE, GRAND CANYON NATIONAL PARK, ARIZONA

Pre-1945, H-4459; $3-5

Pre-1945, H-4473; $4-6

H-4473   COFFEE SHOP, BRIGHT ANGEL LODGE, GRAND CANYON NATIONAL PARK, ARIZONA

Pre-1915, Fred Harvey, Hand-colored No. 1619; $6-8

Hopi House

When the Hopi House was constructed adjacent to the El Tovar and opened in 1905, it was the first curio shop at the Grand Canyon. It was designed by renowned architect Mary Colter, one of the first American architects to appreciate the utility and beauty of Native American design. The original building is an actual re-creation of Hopi dwellings found in and around the Hopi village of Oraibi, Arizona. Following Hopi architectural traditions, the building was constructed primarily by Hopi workmen using native stone and wood.

The view of the El Tovar Hotel from the rooftop of Hopi House. Pre-1945, H-1510; $4-6

H-1510   HOTEL EL TOVAR, GRAND CANYON NATIONAL PARK, ARIZONA

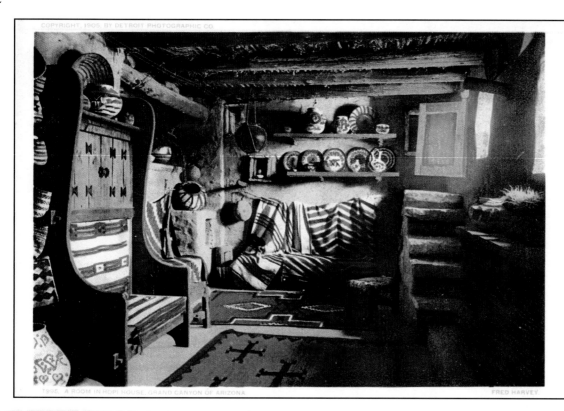

COPYRIGHT, 1905, BY DETROIT PHOTOGRAPHIC CO.

7995. A ROOM IN HOPI HOUSE, GRAND CANYON OF ARIZONA. FRED HARVEY

Pre-1907, Fred Harvey 7995; $5-7

79438 MAIN SALESROOM, HOPI HOUSE, GRAND CANYON, ARIZONA. FRED HARVEY

Pre-1930, Fred Harvey Phostint 79438; $4-6

Pre-1907, Detroit Publishing Company 9289; $5-7

A view of the famous Hopi potter Nampeyo and her family. The Harvey Company hired Nampeyo to live and work at Hopi House in the early 1900s for the benefit of Grand Canyon visitors. Nampeyo was allowed to sell her pottery as tourist pieces. Pre-1915, Fred Harvey 9286; $7-9

Pre-1915, Fred Harvey Phostint 79441; $5-7

74

Pre-1945, H-4466; $4-6

H-4466—Navajo Silversmith, Grand Canyon National Park, Arizona

Nampeyo, Hopi potter, and her family on the roof of the Hopi House, 1905.
Pre-1907, Detroit Publishing Company 9287; $7-9

9287. A NATIVE ROOF GARDEN PARTY, HOPI HOUSE, GRAND CANYON OF ARIZONA.   COPYRIGHT, 1905, BY DETROIT PHOTOGRAPHIC CO.

An altar in the Hopi House at Grand Canyon, constructed by the early Hopi inhabitants. Pre-1915, Fred Harvey Phostint 10987; $5-7

10987 ALTAR, HOPI HOUSE, GRAND CANYON, ARIZONA.   FRED HARVEY.

H-1290   HOPI BASKET WEAVERS, HOPI HOUSE. GRAND CANYON. ARIZONA

Pre-1930, H-1290; $4-6

H-4221   A HOPI POTTERY MAKER, GRAND CANYON NATIONAL PARK, ARIZONA

Pre-1945, H-4221; $4-6

Hermit's Rest, constructed in 1914, is located several miles west of El Tovar Hotel. The building, originally built as a rest stop for the short stage line that ran from the hotel to this location now serves as gift shop and refreshment stand. Pre-1930; $3-4

HERMIT'S REST, GRAND CANYON NATIONAL PARK, ARIZONA.

The Buffalo Dance of the Hopi Indians, being performed for tourists outside the Hopi House. Pre-1930, Fred Harvey Phostint H-3630; $5-7

BUFFALO DANCE OF THE HOPI INDIANS, GRAND CANYON NATIONAL PARK, ARIZONA.   (IN FRONT OF HOPI HOUSE)

H-1537   THE PORCH AT HERMIT'S REST, GRAND CANYON NATIONAL PARK, ARIZONA

Pre-1930, Phostint, H-1537; $5-7

H-1487   THE FIRE PLACE, HERMIT'S REST, GRAND CANYON NATIONAL PARK, ARIZONA.

Pre-1930, Phostint H-1487; $5-7

H-3152   THE ARCH AT HERMIT'S REST, GRAND CANYON NATIONAL PARK, ARIZONA.

Pre-1930, Phostint, H-3162; $4-6

78

H-1890. TELESCOPE IN THE LOOKOUT, GRAND CANYON NATIONAL PARK, ARIZONA.

Pre-1930, H-1890; $5-7

THE LOOKOUT, GRAND CANYON NATIONAL PARK, ARIZONA.
78904

The Lookout Studio is a small Mary Colter-designed structure located along the canyon rim in the vicinity of the Bright Angel Lodge. The building was constructed for tourist viewing of the canyon. Pre-1930; $3-4

Pre-1930, Fred Harvey, unnumbered; $4-6

A CORNER IN THE LOOKOUT, GRAND CANYON, ARIZONA.

H-4219 THE WATCHTOWER AT DESERT VIEW, GRAND CANYON NATIONAL PARK, ARIZONA

Pre-1945, H-4219; $3-5

"THE WATCHTOWER AND THE COLORADO RIVER"—DESERT VIEW, GRAND CANYON NATIONAL PARK, ARIZONA.   FROM PAINTING BY GUNNAR WIDFORSS.

Pre-1930, H-4481; $3-4

The Indian Watchtower at Desert View, completed in 1932, is considered to be one of Mary Colter's architectural masterpieces and was her final project at Grand Canyon. Modeled after a prehistoric tower, the structure is at the eastern end of the south rim of the Grand Canyon. The interior is decorated with paintings by noted Hopi painter, Fred Kabotie.

Pre-1945, Real photo; $6-8

Pre-1945, Real photo; $6-8

H-4223 SNAKE ALTAR IN THE WATCHTOWER, DESERT VIEW, GRAND CANYON NATIONAL PARK, ARIZONA

Pre-1945, H-4223; $4-6

Pre-1945, H-4220; $3-4

H-4220 THE KIVA, DESERT VIEW, GRAND CANYON NATIONAL PARK, ARIZONA

H-3145 A PARTY ON BRIGHT ANGEL TRAIL, GRAND CANYON NATIONAL PARK, ARIZONA.

The Bright Angel Trail at Grand Canyon was originally a trail used by the Havasupai Indians. Ralph Cameron improved the Indian trail in 1880 and began charging $1 to use it. It was known as Cameron's Trail until 1937 when the National Park Service gave it the current name. The trail descends 4380 feet in elevation, from the rim to the Colorado River. Pre-1930, Phostint H-3145; $5-7

Pre-1915, Fred Harvey 5203; $5-7

Pre-1915, Hand-colored H-2368; $8-10

5203. Jacob's Ladder on Bright Angel Trail,
Grand Canyon, Arizona.

© FRED HARVEY

GRAND CANYON, ARIZONA   NATIONAL PARK

H-1505. LOOKING DOWN CATHEDRAL STAIRS ON HERMIT TRAIL

Pre-1930, Phostint H-1505; $5-7

H-3251 THE TOWERING CLIFFS ABOVE HERMIT CAMP, GRAND CANYON NATIONAL PARK, ARIZONA.

The Hermit Trail, like many other Grand Canyon trails, began as an Indian route. The trail was improved by prospectors and was originally know as Horsethief Trail. A prospector by the name of Dan Hogan began construction of the modern Hermit Trail in 1896. The trail was further improved by the Santa Fe Railroad about a decade and a half later. They constructed a small camp, Hermit Camp, at the end of the trail, near where Hermit Creek cuts through a platform and descends to meet the Colorado River. Hermit Camp provided a stopover point for parties headed for the river and was active until the 1930's. Pre-1930, H-3251; $6-8

H-2862 Kaibab Suspension Bridge Across Colorado River, Grand Canyon National Park. (Copyrighted by Fred Harvey)

The Kaibab Suspension Bridge over the Colorado River was constructed in 1928, replacing the earlier Kaibab Trail footbridge (1920). Pre-1930, H-2862; $5-7

H-3963 PHANTOM RANCH, "IN THE LAND OF LIGHT AND SHADOW", GRAND CANYON NATIONAL PARK, ARIZONA

Phantom Ranch, designed by Mary Colter in 1922, is a small, unique resort with rustic cabins at the bottom of the Grand Canyon. Pre-1945, H-3963; $3-4

Chapter 5

Native Americans in the Southwest

Picture postcards played a primary role in marketing strategies by the Santa Fe and Fred Harvey Companies. Fred Harvey's interest in postcard publication began about 1900, and by 1903 the Harvey Company was distributing high-quality, color postcards at newsstands and hotels along the Santa Fe route. At that time, most of the images and the postcard production came from the Detroit Publishing Company, which had a contract to produce postcards for Fred Harvey between 1901 and 1932. After 1907, the Detroit Publishing Company used the Phostint process, a time-consuming and complicated color lithography process that resulted in cards that were exquisite and brightly colored. The Fred Harvey Company continued to publish postcards into the 1960s, but the heyday of Harvey postcards occurred during the first three decades of the twentieth century.

Although Fred Harvey published postcards that included views of places all along the Santa Fe Route, the majority were of sites in New Mexico and Arizona. Included in the postcard inventory were landscape views of the abundant natural wonders found in the Southwest, pictures of the various hotels and other Harvey facilities, and images of the Santa Fe trains crossing mountain passes, the desert, and trestles over deep canyons. The largest portion of Harvey postcard subjects portrays people and scenes associated with the various Native American groups then extant in the American Southwest. These included the twenty or so Pueblo villages in New Mexico, the Hopi pueblos in Arizona, the Navajo of northeastern Arizona, Apache tribes in both states, and smaller tribes located along the Colorado River in Arizona.

13977. FRANCISCO ARESA, CASIQUE OF COCHITI.   FRED HARVEY.

Francisco Aresa, Casique [chief] of Cochiti. Pre-1915,
Fred Harvey Phostint 13977; $7-9

INDIAN BUILDING. ALBUQUERQUE, N. M.

10933 JUANA MARIE, A PUEBLO INDIAN OF ISLETA,   COPR. KARL E. MOON & CO.

The corporate trademarks of both companies claimed to have Native American origins, as trains were named with Indian themes and hotels were designed and decorated with Indian elements. Promotional ads, literature, calendars, playing cards, and timetables emphasized the marketability and display aspects of Southwestern Indian cultures.

The Fred Harvey Company brought Southwestern Indian life and culture to the tourists by having "live" Native Americans present at some hotels to display the manufacture of their material culture. In doing so, the company made some individuals celebrities to the rest of the country, such as the Hopi potter Nampeyo, San Ildefonso Pueblo potter Maria Martinez, and Elle of Ganado, a noted Navajo rug weaver. Each of these artisans appeared on several postcard images as well and attended various world's fairs and regional expositions on behalf of Fred Harvey and the Santa Fe. On the Indian Detours, run by the Harvey Company, tourists were taken directly to the Indians' pueblos where they could witness dances, purchase pottery, and mingle with the native population. An important component of the lasting legacy of the Fred Harvey Company in the Southwest is the variety and beauty expressed in the Harvey postcards portraying the region's Native American peoples and their lifeways. This chapter offers a partial portfolio of Fred Harvey Southwestern Indian images.

Juana Marie, a Pueblo Indian of Isleta [Karl E. Moon Photograph]. Pre-1915, Fred Harvey Phostint 10933; $10-12

Making pottery, Pueblo of San Ildefonso, New Mexico [an early image of Maria Martinez]. Pre-1930, Phostint H-3545; $7-9

H-3545   MAKING POTTERY, PUEBLO OF SAN ILDEFONSO, NEW MEXICO.

85

Published by Fred. Harvey.

TRADE MARK

Fred Harvey

THE GIANT MESSENGER, SANTA FE FIESTA.   From a Painting by Gerald Cassidy.

The Giant Messenger, Santa Fe Fiesta, from a painting by Gerald Cassidy. Pre-1930, H-2920; $8-10

79826 OLD MEDICINE MAN, PUEBLO OF TESUQUE, N. M.

Old medicine man, Pueblo of Tesuque, New Mexico. Pre-1915, Fred Harvey Phostint 79826; $5-7

86

Cochiti Indian in Buffalo Dance.
Pre-1915, Detroit Publishing
Company Phostint 71275; $5-7

Indian men in ceremonial dancing
costume, Pueblo of Santo Domingo,
near Thornton, New Mexico.
Pre-1930, Phostint H-2072; $6-8

A woman of Isleta Pueblo.
Pre-1907, Detroit Publishing
Company 5889; $6-8

Winnowing grain, Pueblo of
Tesuque, New Mexico. Pre-1915,
Fred Harvey Phostint 79828; $6-8

Pueblo Indian drilling turquoise,
New Mexico. Pre-1915, Fred
Harvey Phostint 13989; $6-8

Pueblo Indian with olla.
Pre-1930. Detroit Publishing
Company Phostint 6503; $6-8

COPR. KARL E. MOON & CO.

10934 LO-LEE-TA, PUEBLO GIRL OF LAGUNA, NEW MEXICO

Lo-Lee-Ta, a Pueblo girl of Laguna, New
Mexico. Pre-1915, Fred Harvey Phostint
10934; $8-10

Indian women of Acoma Pueblo, New Mexico.
Pre-1915, Detroit Publishing Company
Phostint 11255; $6-8

The first riding lesson. Pre-1915,
Fred Harvey Phostint 14930; $5-7

Interior of House of Isleta
Pueblo. Pre-1915, Fred
Harvey Phostint 10992;
$6-8

90

Grinding corn, Pueblo of Laguna, New Mexico. Pre-1915, Detroit Publishing Company 11707; $ 5-7

11707 GRINDING CORN, PUEBLO OF LAGUNA, N. M.

12219 CHILDREN OF INDIAN PUEBLO OF LAGUNA, N. M.

Children of Indian Pueblo of Laguna, New Mexico. Pre-1915, Detroit Publishing Company 12219; $6-8

An afternoon call, Pueblo of Laguna, New Mexico. Pre-1915, Detroit Publishing Company 71091; $6-8

71091 AN AFTERNOON CALL, PUEBLO OF LAGUNA, NEW MEXICO

The estufa, Corn Dance, Pueblo of Santo Domingo, New Mexico. Pre-1915, Fred Harvey Phostint 12954; $5-7

Drying peaches at Isleta, New Mexico. Pre-1915, Detroit Publishing Company Phostint 11279; $6-8

A woman of Pueblo of Isleta decorating pottery. Pre-1915, Fred Harvey Phostint 11968; $5-7

Navajo chicken pull. Pre-1915, Detroit
Publishing Company 71272; $6-8

Navajo Indians gambling, Arizona. Pre-1915,
Fred Harvey Phostint 10993; $6-8

Navajo woman on the reservation, Arizona. Fred Harvey, Hand-colored, No. 385; $10-12

Navajo woman and
papoose, New Mexico.
Pre-1915, Phostint
H-1953; $6-8

H-1953. NAVAHO WOMAN AND PAPOOSE, NEW MEXICO

Pedro, a Navajo [Karl E. Moon photograph]. Pre-1915,
Fred Harvey Phostint 10930; $6-8.

A Pueblo woman
and child.
Pre-1915, Fred
Harvey Phostint
79215; $5-7

79215 A PUEBLO WOMAN AND CHILD.   FRED HARVEY

94

Elle of Ganado, acknowledged the best weaver among the Navajo. Pre-1916, Fred Harvey Phostint 9996; $7-9

Tom of Ganado, Indian Building, Albuquerque, New Mexico. Pre-1915, Fred Harvey Phostint 10936; $7-9

An old Navajo Indian medicine man, New Mexico. Pre-1915, Fred Harvey Phostint 79905; $6-8

NAVAHO BOY.   FRED HARVEY.

COPYRIGHT 1906 BY KARL E. MOON & CO.

Navajo boy [Karl E. Moon photograph].
Pre-1907, Fred Harvey, unnumbered; $14-16

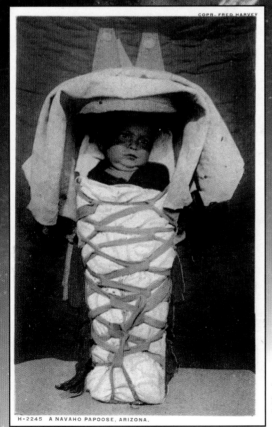

H-2245 A NAVAHO PAPOOSE, ARIZONA.

A Navajo Indian
silversmith, New
Mexico. Pre-1930,
Phostint H-2383; $6-8

A Navajo Papoose,
Arizona. Pre-1930,
Phostint H-2245; $5-7

H-2383 A NAVAHO INDIAN SILVERSMITH, NEW MEXICO.

96

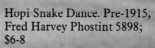

Hopi Snake Dance. Pre-1915,
Fred Harvey Phostint 5898;
$6-8

Taqui, a Hopi (Moki) Snake Priest. Pre-1915, Detroit Publishing
Company 5886; $10-12

Hopi snake hunters returning
at sunset. Pre-1915, Detroit
Publishing Company 11280; $6-8

A Hopi Indian wood train, Arizona.
Pre-1915, Fred Harvey Phostint 79245;
$6-8

Carrying water to Tewa,
Arizona. Pre-1915, Fred
Harvey Phostint 79450; $6-8

Supai woman weaving
basket, Cataract
Canyon, Arizona.
Pre-1915, Fred Harvey
Phostint 10983; $7-9

5244 MOKI INDIAN CIGARETTE SMOKER

Moki [Hopi]
Indian cigarette
smoker.
Pre-1915,
Detroit
Publishing
Company 5244;
$7-9

79490 HOPI CIGARETTE SMOKER   FRED HARVEY

Hopi cigarette
smoker.
Pre-1915,
Fred Harvey
Phostint
79490; $7-9

0980.   HOPI ANGA KATCINA, ARIZONA.   FRED HARVEY.

Hopi Anga
Katcina,
Arizona.
Prc-1915,
Fred Harvey
Phostint
10980; $7-9

10981   HOPI SHOOYOKOS KATCINA ARIZONA   COPYRIGHT 1906 BY FRED HARVEY

Hopi Shooyokos
Katcina, Arizona.
Pre-1915, Fred
Harvey Phostint
10981; $10-12

Nampeyo (the noted Hopi pottery maker) and her grandchild. Pre-1915, Detroit Publishing Company 12220; $10-12

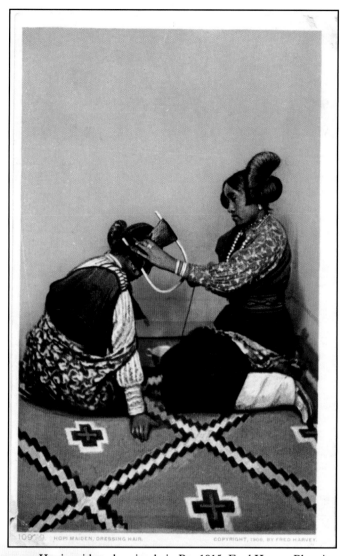

Hopi maiden, dressing hair. Pre-1915, Fred Harvey Phostint 10979; $7-9

Old basket weaver and daughter, Hopi (Moki) Pueblo. Pre-1915, Detroit Publishing Company 70725; $7-9

100

5890 "THE MAN WITH THE HOE, MOKI PUEBLO.

The man with the hoe, Moki [Hopi] Pueblo.
Pre-1915, Detroit Publishing Company
5890; $6-8

13395 BRINGING IN THE HARVEST, "HOPI PUEBLOS." COPR. DETROIT PUBLISHING CO.

Bringing in the harvest, Hopi Pueblos. Pre-1915,
Detroit Publishing Company 13395; $7-9

10958. HOPI BASKET WEAVER, PUEBLO OF MISHONGNAVI, ARIZONA. FRED HARVEY.

Hopi basket weaver, Pueblo of Mishongnavi, Arizona.
Pre-1915, Fred Harvey Phostint 10958; $7-9

A Hopi Thanksgiving, Pueblo of
Oraibi, Arizona. Pre-1915, Detroit
Publishing Company 11248; $6-8

Hopi Indian bread carrier.
Pre-1915, Detroit Publishing
Company 71274; $7-9

Hopi maiden grinding corn.
Pre-1915, Fred Harvey Phostint
14912; $7-9

Hopi mending moccasins.
Pre-1915, Detroit Publishing
Company Phostint 11262; $7-9

Apache warriors at Rio Navajo, Arizona. Pre-1915, Photostint H-2014; $6-8

Apache Warriors. Pre-1915, Detroit Publishing Company 5242; $7-9

Apaches halting for water at Rio Navajo, Arizona. Pre-1915, Fred Harvey Phostint 13944; $6-8

A Jicarilla Apache Chief, Arizona. Pre-1915, Fred Harvey Phostint 13942; $7-9

Buffalo Calf, Jicarilla Apache, Arizona. Pre-1915, Fred Harvey Phostint 13943; $7-9

13941 MONTERA CABEZON, AN APACHE INDIAN, ARIZONA. COPR. FRED HARVEY

Montera Cabezon, an Apache Indian, Arizona.
Pre-1915, Fred Harvey Phostint 13941; $7-9

11971 MOJAVE INDIANS GAMBLING, NEEDLES, CALIF. FRED HARVEY

Mojave Indians Gambling, Needles, California.
Pre-1915, Fred Harvey Phostint 11971; $6-8

11256   AN APACHE CHIEF IN CAMP   DETROIT PUBLISHING CO.

An Apache chief in camp. Pre-1915, Detroit
Publishing Company Phostint 11256; $7-9

⭘ Chapter 6
Expositions To Promote The Southwest

The Santa Fe and Fred Harvey Companies organized promotional exhibits at several national and international expositions, including the World's Columbian Exposition in 1893 in Chicago and the 1904 Louisiana Purchase Exposition in St. Louis. In 1915, they produced significant exhibits for two contemporaneous California expositions, the Panama-Pacific International Exposition in San Francisco and the Panama-California Exposition held in San Diego. The San Diego experience, held at Balboa Park in honor of the opening of the Panama Canal, is instructive of the level of effort and attention to detail that the Santa Fe and Fred Harvey put into their exhibits.

The Southwestern exhibit at San Diego was called "The Painted Desert," after the scenic area along the train route in eastern Arizona. It was staffed with nearly 200 Native Americans from eight Southwestern tribes: Apache, Navajo, Havasupai from the Grand Canyon, and the pueblos of Hopi, Acoma, Isleta,

San Ildefonso, and Taos. The Painted Desert compound was dominated by a multi-storied and terraced Southwestern pueblo, modeled after the villages of Zuni and Taos in New Mexico where the Pueblo people lived. At the opposite side of the compound lived the desert peoples, the Apache in dome-shaped wickiups, the Navajo in hogans, and the Havasupai in brush-covered shacks with dirt-covered roofs. Between them was a full-size representation of a prehistoric cliff house situated in a cliff of fake rocks to represent the ancestors of the pueblo peoples.

H-1037   PUEBLO VILLAGE, "THE PAINTED DESERT", SAN DIEGO, CALIF.   PANAMA-CALIFORNIA EXPOSITION

Circa 1915; H-1037; $7-9

106

Circa 1915; H-1035; $7-9

Circa 1915; H-1032; $7-9

Circa 1915; Fred Harvey
No. 869; $10-12

107

Circa 1915; Fred Harvey No 877; $10-12

Pueblo Indians Baking Pottery, The Painted Desert. International Panama-California Exposition, San Diego, California.

Circa 1915; Real photo; $10-12

Cliff Dwellers "Painted Deserts" — San Diego, Calif.

International Panama-California Exposition, San Diego, California. Portion of the Pueblo Village, The Painted Desert.

Circa 1915; Fred Harvey No. 874; $10-12

Circa 1915; Fred Harvey No. 878; $10-12

Circa 1915; Fred Harvey No. 870; $10-12

International Panama-California Exposition, San Diego, California.
NAVAHOS CARDING AND SPINNING WOOL AND WEAVING A BLANKET.
THE PAINTED DESERT.

Circa 1915; Fred Harvey No. 875; $10-12

Navaho Blanket Weaver
"The Painted Desert"–San Diego, Calif

Circa 1915; Real photo; $10-12

Pueblo Village
"The Painted Desert" — San Diego, Calif.

Circa 1915; Real photo; $10-12

H-1036   MAKING POTTERY, "THE PAINTED DESERT", SAN DIEGO, CALIF.
PANAMA-CALIFORNIA EXPOSITION

The San Diego Exposition opened in Balboa Park in January of 1915, and closed about two years later. During the Exposition, the paticipating Native Americans lived at the compound, performed dances for the spectators, and otherwise enjoyed a relatively normal life far from their homes. Maria Martinez of San Ildefonso Pueblo made pottery with sacks of clay and sand brought from her native village in New Mexico. Hopi women cooked corn, squash, and mutton. They hung peppers, fruits, and vegetables from overhangs of buildings and worked and played in the pueblo plaza. Here, they also cooked over fireplaces and in bread ovens and herded cattle, sheep, goats, and horses into corrals – all transported from their Arizona or New Mexico homelands, courtesy of the Santa Fe Railway.

After the exposition closed, the Painted Desert Pueblo was converted into quarters for the U.S. Army during World War I. In 1920, the San Diego County Council of Boy Scouts took possession of the Indian village and held it until 1941, with the exception of a brief period in 1935-1936 when it was used for the California-Pacific International Exposition. The compound was taken over by the military in 1941 as a headquarters and supply depot for anti-aircraft batteries along the coast during World War II. The U.S. Army moved out in 1946 and the San Diego Fire Department burned down the wood and stucco structures that were still standing.

Maria Martinez of San Ildefonso Pueblo in New Mexico is shown in this image molding pottery vessels. After decoration and firing, the pottery was traded to the exhibit's trading post for clothes, food, and money, and later sold to the visiting public. Circa 1915; H-1036; $12-14

Another view of Maria Martinez firing pottery at the San Diego Painted Desert Exhibit. In years to come, Maria would become one of the most celebrated Indian potters, having a worldwide reputation for her artistry. She passed away at her village of San Ildefonso, New Mexico, in 1980. Circa 1915; Fred Harvey No. 876; $14-16

International Panama - California Exposition, San Diego, California.
Pueblo Indian Firing Pottery, The Painted Desert.

No. 876.

The Indian Village

The Painted Desert Exhibit Indian Pueblo as it looked during the 1935-36 California-Pacific International Exposition. Circa 1935; Real photo; $7-9

Additional Reading

Berke, Arnold. *Mary Colter: Architect of the Southwest.* New York, New York, Princeton Architectural Press, 2002.

Bryant, Keith L., Jr. *History of the Atchison, Topeka and Santa Fe Railway.* New York, New York, Macmillon Publishing Company, Inc., 1974.

D'Emilio, Sandra and Susan Campbell. *Visions and Visionaries: The Art and Artists of the Santa Fe Railway.* Layton, Utah, Gibbs-Smith Publisher, 1991.

Dilworth, Leah. *Imagining Indians in the Southwest: Persistent Visions of a Primitive Past.* Washington, District of Columbia, Smithsonian Institution Press, 1996.

Dye, Victoria E. *All Aboard for Santa Fe: Railway Promotion of the Southwest, 1890s to 1930s.* Albuquerque, New Mexico, University of New Mexico Press, 2005.

Harmon, Don. *Postcard History of the Early Santa Fe Railway.* Shawnee Mission, Kansas, Harmon Publishing Company, 2006.

Howard, Kathleen L., and Diana F. Pardue. *Inventing the Southwest: The Fred Harvey Company and Native American Art.* Flagstaff, Arizona, Northland Publishing, 1996.

Manchester, Albert D. *Trails Begin Where Rails End: Early-day Motoring Adventures in the West and Southwest.* Glendale, California, Trans-Anglo Books, 1987.

Marshall, James. *Santa Fe, The Railroad That Built an Empire.* New York, New York, Random House, 1945.

McCall, John B. *Dining and Beverage Service Cars of the Santa Fe – Featuring Service by Fred Harvey.* Midwest City, Oklahoma, The Santa Fe Railway Historical and Modeling Society, 2006.

McLuhan, T.C. *Dream Tracks: The Railroad and the American Indian, 1890-1930.* New York, New York, Harry N. Abrams, Inc., 1985.

Myrick, David F. *New Mexico's Railroads: An Historical Survey.* Golden, Colorado, Colorado Railroad Museum, 1970.

Myrick, David F. *The Santa Fe Route: Railroads of Arizona, Volume 4.* Wilton, California, Signature Press, 1998.

Poling-Kempes, Lesley. *The Harvey Girls: Women Who Opened the West.* New York, New York, Paragon House, 1989.

Thomas, Diane H. *The Southwestern Indian Detours.* Phoenix, Arizona, Hunter Publishing Company, 1978.

Weigle, Marta and Barbara A. Babcock. *The Great Southwest of the Fred Harvey Company and the Santa Fe Railway.* Phoenix, Arizona, The Heard Museum, 1996.

Panama-Pacific International Exposition, San Francisco, California.

Santa Fe's Grand Canyon Exhibit.

Trail looking East, Indian Village

The 1915 Panama-Pacific International Exposition in San Francisco, California, ran concurrent with the Panama-California Exposition in San Diego. The Santa Fe Railway and Fred Harvey also sponsored a Native American exhibit, called the "Grand Canyon Exhibit," that included a constructed Southwestern Indian village. Circa 1915; Fred Harvey No. 1064; $10-12

Index